JOS

# CONCERTO

for Harpsichord (Piano) and Orchestra
D major/D-Dur/Ré majeur
Hob. XVIII: 11
Edited by/Herausgegeben von
Kurt Soldan

## Ernst Eulenburg Ltd
London · Mainz · New York · Paris · Tokyo · Zürich

Reprinted by permission of C. F. Peters Corporation,
New York, and Hinrichsen Edition Ltd, London
© 1931 C. F. Peters

# Haydn, Piano Concerto D major

Among Haydn's numerous Piano Concertos only the one in G major and in D major appeared in print, and even among those two only the latter reached a special popularity, so that it could see more frequent prints. Artaria announced it in 1784 with the explicit remark: " The only Piano Concerto of Haydn, which so far has appeared in print." As pattern the Mainz Edition No. 7 (Schott) was used, this again is " copié d'après le Journal de Pièces de Clavecin de Mons. Boyer à Paris." In March, 1785, also Torricella announced this Concerto " von dem berühmten Herrn Joseph Haydn." No autographed MS. has so far been found of the score, the solo, or the orchestra parts. The edition here presented, being the first engraved print is in particular based on written parts from the end of the 18th century owned by the Preussische Staats - Bibliothek, which, as it seems from the faults— f.i. the Horns are exchanged—may have been the precursor of the first printed edition. Moreover were used the prints of Schott and Artaria, both published during Haydn's life-time, the latter of which shows the following title:

# Haydn, Klavier-Konzert D dur

Von allen Klavier - Konzerten Haydns erschienen nur das in G dur und D dur im Druck, und auch von diesen erlangte nur das letztere besondere Beliebtheit, sodass es sogar häufigere Auflagen erlebte. Artaria kündigte es 1784 ausdrücklich mit dem Beisatz an: " Das einzige Klavier-Konzert Haydns, das bisher im Stich erschienen ist." Als Vorlage diente ihm die Mainzer Ausgabe No. 7 (Schott), diese wiederum ist " copié d'après le Journal de pièces de Clavecin de Mons. Boyer à Paris." Im März 1785 kündigte auch Torricella dieses Konzert "von dem berühmten Herrn Joseph Haydn" an. Ein Autograph der Partitur, der Solostimme oder Orchesterstimmen ist bisher noch nicht aufgetaucht. Die vorliegende, zum ersten Male gestochene Partitur-Ausgabe stützt sich vor allem auf eine im Besitz der Preussischen Staats-Bibliothek befindliche Stimmenhandschrift aus dem Ende des 18. Jahrhunderts, die, den Fehlern nach zu urteilen, (u.a. sind die Hörner im Finale vertauscht) wohl als Vorläufer der ersten gedruckten Ausgabe zu betrachten ist. Hinzugezogen wurden ferner die noch zu Haydns Lebzeiten erschienenen Ausgaben von Schott und Artaria, welch letztere folgenden Titel zeigt:

Concerto
Per il
Clavicembalo ó Forte piano
Con l'Acommpagnamento
Di Due Violini, Viola, Due Oboi,
Due Corni
E Basso
Composto dal Sig^e.
GIUSEPPE HAYDN
Maestro di Capella di S. A.
il Principe d'Esterhazy &
Opera XXIXVII
In Vienne presso Artaria Compag^e.

In all these editions the Solo part contains but very few dynamic signs, while expression and dynamic signs of orchestra parts are so careless as can be after the use of that time: much particulars are dealt with as a matter of course, even as unimportant, which do no more appear as irrelevant today.

To make this Concerto, composed for Cembalo with a small (Chamber-) orchestra, being most attractive and to be considered as a genuine Haydn, again accessible to the Harpischordists of our time, no modern additions or alterations were undertaken. Only evident writing or engraving faults have been rectified, and this again in all doubtful cases been made visible by smaller engraving types.

KURT SOLDAN.

Concerto
Per il
Clavicembalo ó Forte piano
Con l'Acommpagnamento
Di Due Violini, Viola, Due Oboi,
Due Corni
E Basso
Composto dal Sig^e.
GIUSEPPE HAYDN
Maestro di Capella di S. A.
il Principe d'Esterhazy &
Opera XXXVII
In Vienne presso Artaria Compag^e.

In allen diesen Vorlagen weist die Solostimme nur sehr wenige dynamische Angaben auf, während die Phrasierungszeichen und dynamische Bezeichnung der Orchesterstimmen so nachlässig sind, wie eben Orchesterstimmen aus ihrer Zeit nur sein können: vieles ist in diesen als selbstverständlich, ja gleichgiltig behandelt, was uns heute nicht mehr nebensächlich erscheint.

Um dieses für Cembalo unter Begleitung eines kleinen (Kammer-) Orchesters komponierte, überaus reizvolle, als échter Haydn anzusprechende Werk den Cembalisten unserer heutigen Zeit wieder zugänglich zu machen, wurde von irgendwelchen modernen Zusätzen oder Anderungen abgesehen. Es sind nur offensichtliche Schreib- und Stichfehler richtiggestellt; und dies wiederum in Zweifelsfällen durch kleineren Stich kenntlich gemacht.

KURT SOLDAN.

# CONCERTO

## I

Joseph Haydn
1732–1809

4

6

E. E. 6006

8

E.E.6006

9

E.E.6006

10

12

E.E.6006

14

16

19

*Cadenza see p.43*

E.E.6006

# II

22

E.E.6006

E.E.6006

26

E.E.6006

Cadenza  p. 44

# III

**Rondo all' Ungherese**

E.E.6006

38
Piano
I
Vl.
II
Vla.
Vc.
eB.
44
Piano
I
Vl.
II
Vla.
Vc
eB.
51
Piano
I
Vl.
II
Vla.
Vc
eB.

E.E.6006

84

E.E.6006

E.E.6006

E.E.6006

E.E.6006

## CADENZA to the 1st Movement. (p. 19)

## CADENZA to the 2nd Movement. (p. 27)